Sinbad the Sailor

Contents

About the story

The stories of Sinbad the Sailor
come from Iraq in the Middle East.
They tell of the seven voyages he made.
He was brave and clever
and lived to be a rich man.
The map shows the seas he sailed.

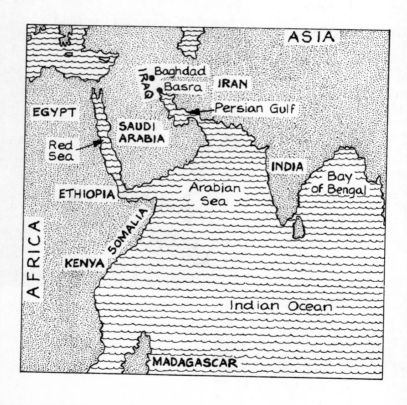

1

Sinbad

Sinbad came from a wealthy family.
They lived in the old city of Baghdad.
Baghdad is in the country
now known as Iraq.

When Sinbad's parents died,
he became a rich young man.
But Sinbad was not rich for long!
He soon spent all his money
having a good time.
He had to sell his house
and everything he owned
to pay his debts.

Sinbad had never had to work in his life.
Now he did not know what to do!
He made up his mind to join a ship
and go to sea.
If he did not make any money,
at least he would see the world.
He thought he might even
have some adventures!

Little did he know that he would
have many adventures.
Often his life would be in great danger.
But, in the end, he would become
the richest man in Baghdad.

2

The Strange Island

Sinbad went to the port of Basra
and joined a ship.
It was a trading ship and it stopped
at many places.
Sinbad and the crew bought and sold
things at every place they visited.
They traded spices such as
pepper and cloves.
They traded cloth such as
silk and fine cotton.
They traded things made of
copper, brass and silver.

After many months the ship was full.
The captain said it was time
to return home.
There they would sell all their goods.
They were going to make a lot of money.

One day the ship came to
a low, green island.
It was smooth and only a few metres high.
Sinbad and some other sailors
jumped on to the island.
They lit a fire and started to cook a meal.

Suddenly the island moved!
It shivered and shook.
Sinbad realised that it was not
an island at all.
It was a huge whale!

The fire had woken the sleeping whale.
It leapt up out of the water.
Then it crashed down into the waves.

Sinbad was thrown into the sea.
He clung to a piece of driftwood.
When he looked round,
the ship was far away.

Sinbad drifted for several days.
Then he was washed up
on the shore of a far country.
When he was found he was taken to the king.
The king looked after Sinbad
and treated him well.

One day, Sinbad's old ship stopped
to trade with the king.
The captain was amazed to see Sinbad.
'We thought the whale had killed you!'
he said. 'We were sure you were dead.'

Sinbad thanked the king for his kindness.
He sailed back home.
The captain of the ship had kept
all of Sinbad's goods.
When he sold them, Sinbad had enough
money to buy a house for himself.

3

The Roc

It was not long before Sinbad set sail again.
After many weeks at sea,
his ship stopped at an island.
The sailors went on shore
to look for fresh water.
Sinbad went too, but he got lost.
When he found his way back to the beach
the ship had gone!

He looked for some way to escape
from the island.
While he was exploring he saw a huge,
round, white rock,
It was smooth and shiny.
Sinbad walked round it.
He was puzzled.

Just then a great shadow fell on the ground.
Sinbad looked up.
To his horror he saw a giant bird
swooping down towards him.
'This isn't a rock,' Sinbad said to himself.
'It's an egg!'

The giant bird was called a Roc.
It settled on the egg.
Sinbad thought of a plan
to get off the island.
But it was risky!

He unwrapped his turban and tied himself
to the Roc's leg.
When the Roc flew away,
it took Sinbad with it.

It flew for several hours over the sea
to a land of high mountains
and rocky cliffs.
It landed in a valley.
Sinbad untied himself
before the bird flew away again.

He looked about him.
The floor of the valley was covered in
diamonds and other precious stones!
But the cliffs on all sides of the valley were
too steep to climb.

'Just my luck!' said Sinbad. 'I've got all
these riches and can't get out!'
But Sinbad soon had other worries.
When evening came, giant snakes slid out
of holes in the rocky cliffs.

Sinbad found a tree and climbed to safety.
He stayed awake all night.
He didn't want to fall asleep
and drop out of the tree.
The snakes would get him!

In the morning the snakes had gone.
Sinbad collected as many diamonds
as he could carry.

Suddenly, there was a loud thump
behind him.
When he turned round he saw a lump
of raw meat on the ground!

He looked up.
At the top of the cliff were some men.
They were throwing lumps of meat down
into the valley.
He saw eagles swoop down
and pick up the meat.
They flew away back to their nests.
Some of the diamonds stuck to the meat.
Then the men scared away the eagles
and collected the valuable stones.

Sinbad called out to the men.
They let down a long rope
and he was able to climb up.
He told them who he was and about the Roc.

Sinbad stayed with the men for a few days.
They told him where he could find
a ship to take him home.

When he got back to Baghdad
he sold his diamonds.
He was now a rich man again.

4

Cannibals

One day Sinbad told his friends
that he was going to sea again.
'Is that wise?' they said. 'You're a rich
man now. Think of the dangers!'
'I know I don't need to go,' said Sinbad,
'but I'm bored.'

And so, once again, Sinbad set sail.
And once again, luck turned against him.
The ship was caught in a terrible storm.
The wind blew away the sails.
Gigantic waves crashed down
on to the deck.
The ship was smashed into little pieces
on a rocky coast.

Only a few of the crew managed
to swim to the shore.
Sinbad was one of them.
The others were all drowned.

'Where are we?' one of the sailors asked.
'I don't know,' said Sinbad,
'but we can't stay here. We need
to find food and shelter.'

They set off to explore.
Soon they had left the rocky coast behind.
They found a great forest.
It was full of strange plants and trees.
The sailors wanted to eat
the fruit on the trees
but Sinbad told them not to.

'In all my travels, I've never seen fruit like this,' he said. 'It might be poisonous.'

'Well, it hasn't poisoned them!'
said one of the sailors.
He pointed to some men who were coming towards them.

The men were carrying spears
but they did not attack Sinbad
and the other sailors.
They spoke a strange language
which Sinbad did not understand.
They made signs to the sailors
to go along with them.

Soon they came to a village.
They brought food out for the sailors.
Sinbad noticed that none of the people
in the village were eating!
'I don't like the look of this,'
he said to himself.
He only pretended to eat.

It was not long before he knew
he had done the right thing.
The other sailors who had eaten went mad!
They rolled their eyes and jumped around,
yelling like wild animals.
Then they sat down with silly grins
on their faces.

'I'd better behave the same way,'
thought Sinbad.
So he did.

Over the next few weeks
the people of the village
brought more and more food
for the sailors.
They got fatter and fatter
Sinbad only pretended to eat.
He stayed as thin as ever.

One by one the sailors disappeared.
Sinbad realised what was happening
to them.
The villagers were cannibals!
When they had fattened the sailors up,
they ate them!
They had left Sinbad until last
because he was so thin.

Sinbad knew he had to escape.
He waited for a chance.
It came when the villagers
went off to gather fruit.
They left one old man to guard him.
They had not tied Sinbad up
because they thought that he was mad
like the other sailors.

Sinbad ran away.
The old man could not catch him.
He was free!

5

Buried Alive

Sinbad travelled for a week.
Then he came to the gates of a city.
He was taken to the king of the city
who asked who he was.

'My name is Sinbad.'
'Ah,' said the king. 'Sinbad the Sailor!
I have heard of you
and your adventures.
You are welcome to stay here.'
Sinbad stayed for many months.

One day, the king sent for him.

19

'You have been a great help to me,'
he said to Sinbad.
'You have brought many ideas
from your world to ours.'

'Your majesty is kind,' said Sinbad.

'I want to reward you,' said the king.
'I want you to marry
the most beautiful of my daughters.
You will have a house and servants.'

Sinbad really wanted to go home
to Baghdad.
But he knew that he could not refuse.

And so he was married.
The king's daughter was beautiful
but she was weak and sickly.
After only a short time she became ill
and died.

Then Sinbad found out
what was going to happen
at the funeral.
He would be buried alive in his wife's grave!
He would be given some bread and water.
When that ran out he would starve!

The terrible day came.
The body of his wife
was lowered into a deep cave.
Then Sinbad was lowered down too.
A great stone was rolled over the entrance.

Sinbad made his bread and water
last as long as he could.
At the end of a week it had all gone.

He sat in the darkness in despair.
He wished he had never left Baghdad.
Then he heard a noise.
And he felt something move behind him.

He jumped to his feet.
He was terrified!
But then, in the gloom, he saw
it was a small animal.

Sinbad decided to kill it and eat it.
The little animal ran away
when he chased it.
It ran into a dark opening in the cave.
Sinbad went after it.

He followed the animal through tunnels
in the rock.

Sometimes he had to squeeze
through narrow passages.
Then he saw a tiny point of daylight!
It was where the little animal
got into the cave.
He scraped away the soil and climbed out
into the daylight.

Sinbad kept away from the city.
He travelled for many weeks.
At last he reached the coast
and found a ship
to take him home.

6

The Last Voyage

Sinbad went on more voyages.
He had many more adventures.
He got into danger but always escaped.
He saw amazing things and became even
richer than before.
But he made up his mind
never to go to sea again.
He was rich enough and too old
to face the dangers.

One day the ruler of Baghdad,
the Caliph, sent for Sinbad.
'I want you to go on a journey,' he said.
'I want you to take a message
to the King of Serendip.'

The last thing that Sinbad wanted
was to go to sea again.
But he could not refuse.

The voyage to the land of Serendip
was peaceful.
Sinbad gave the Caliph's message
to the king who was pleased.
He gave Sinbad many presents.

On the voyage home, Sinbad's ship
was attacked by pirates!
They took him back to their land.

'We have heard of you,' the leader
of the pirates said. 'If you help us,
we will let you go home.'
'I do not have any choice,' said Sinbad.
'What do you want me to do?'

He told Sinbad that wild elephants
had been attacking them.

'We want you to kill the elephants,'
said the chief.

They took Sinbad into the jungle.
They gave him a great bow and arrows.
Sinbad climbed up a tree
and waited for the elephants.

He did not have to wait long.
The ground shook
and a great herd of elephants
gathered round the tree.

Sinbad tried to draw the bow.
But he was so afraid his hands shook.

The largest of the elephants
took hold of Sinbad
with its trunk.
It swung him on to its back.
Then all the elephants moved off.

Sinbad clung to the elephant.
He wondered where it was taking him.

At last they came to a clearing
Sinbad could hardly believe his eyes!
Everywhere he looked he saw the bones
and tusks of dead elephants.

'This must be the famous graveyard
of the elephants!' he gasped.
Then he knew why the elephants
had taken him there.

He spoke to the largest elephant.
'The people hunt you
for your ivory tusks,' Sinbad said.
'Is that why you attack them?'
The great elephant nodded.

'Can they take this ivory?' Sinbad asked.
The elephant nodded again.
'Then they will not need to hunt you,
and you will not attack them!'

The elephants took Sinbad back.
He told the pirate chief
about the elephants' graveyard.
The people stopped hunting the elephants.

Sinbad was given a ship full of ivory.
He returned to Baghdad.
He sold the ivory.
It made him the richest man in the city.

Sinbad lived happily for many more years.
But he never went to sea again!